The Dark Side of My Mind

Volume 6

Briana Blair

The Dark Side of My Mind Volume 6

ISBN 978-0-557-76134-0

Contact me: webmaster@bluedragoncreations.com

Visit my website: http://bluedragoncreations.com/gallery/

Table of Contents

Frigid - November 1996

Frigid fingers

Touching

Tearing

Frozen bits

Falling

Shattering

Icicle blood

Dripping freezing

Dripping falling

Shattered shards

Falling falling

Clicking slickly

Dripping falling

Melting pooling

Mass of purest nothing

Dripping running

Running gone

Misery: Part 2 - November 1996

Misery

Running

Dripping out of

Once honey covered spaces

Dreamy places

Wishful thoughts

It disgraces

Making murky

Dark and blurry

My memory spaces

The few good places

Found through the years

Amidst the tears

And fears

I'm weak

It's bleak

Misery consumes

Misery resumes

Its place at the head of the table

The Table - November 1996

The table's set

The guests are here

Or seem to be.

Who they are

Shall we see?

Misery heads the table

The reaper to the right

The fates to her left.

In the seat just past

Ole Satan wears a grin.

At the other end am I

Unhappy and afraid

Staring at the empty chairs.

But they have always been

One for my lover

And one for my savior.

But we never see them here

For theses evils are my family

With whom I do reside

And at this table mother misery

Will keep me 'til I die.

Maine - *November 1996*

The grass

Brown

The leaves

Down

The winds

Whistling

Cold air

Bristling

Frigid air

Frozen there

Snow is snowing

Winds are blowing

Trudging through snow

Wherever you go

Scraping the ice

Is not so nice

That's life in Maine

What a pain

Words - ***November 1996***

From where do the words come?

To where do the words go?

The words that help

The words that hurt

The words that are my life.

To whom are the words said?

By whom are the words heard?

The words that sing

The words that cry

These words that are my life.

Why are the words here?

Why are the words mine?

These words that come

These words that be

These words that are my life.

Words: Part 2 - November 1996

They are

They be

Alive

Through me

They come

They are

Both near

And far

They live

They thrive

They will

Survive

When I

Am gone

They will

Live on

For words

Are timeless

And true

Who Am I? - November 1996

Who am I?

The one whose wishes are denied.

I, the one to whom is lied.

Who am I?

The one whose face is marred.

I, the one whose heart is scarred.

Who am I?

The one whose soul is lost.

I, the one who has been crossed.

Who am I?

I am no one in this place.

No one, just a soul without a face.

Hope - November 1996

Why live,

Why go on,

When there is nothing?

Why care,

Why try,

When there is no one?

Why,

When there is no hope?

Why,

When time takes all you've got?

Why,

When life gives nothing back?

Why,

When there is no hope?

Fading - November 1996

Fading,

Disappearing,

Like a sunset,

But not so graceful.

Just weakening,

Faltering,

Soon to be gone.

Not loved,

Not missed,

Not remembered,

Just faded,

And gone.

Thanksgiving - November 1996

It's Thanksgiving,

But what is there to give thanks for?

There's snow on the ground,

And the heat's almost gone.

The cupboards look bare,

'Cause the food's almost gone.

The bills aren't paid,

'Cause the money's all gone.

There's nothing to live for,

'Cause our hope is gone.

What's there to give thanks for

With no hope in sight?

We could only give thanks

If we died tonight.

Away - *November 1996*

I'd like to get away

From this place

From this body

Far away

To be free

And unencumbered

To a place

Undefined

But away

Far away

Where my soul can breathe

And my body can rest

And my mind can be free again

Alien - December 1996

I don't belong here

I am an alien

You look like me

You talk like me

You act like me

But you are not like me

And I am not like you

I am an alien

Grasping onto hope and dreams

Floating through a strange world

This place is not mine

You are not mine

Nothing is mine

And I'm alone on this planet

Searching for others like me

With dreams and plans and goodness

A thing more alien here than I

And the alien that is I

Shall conquer the dark solitude

And become greater than they

And shape them in my image.

Tears - December 1996

Tears

So many tears

That fall

Like eternal rain

My eyes ache

And I taste the salty sting

Of my only companions

Pain has become a resident

In this dying body of mine

And the tears flow

Perhaps to make the river

In which I can drown

Glorious Death - *December 1996*

Oh, glorious death

Save me from my pain

Take me from this evil place

That's driving me insane

Oh, glorious death

Kill this horrid shell

Release me from this body

That is my living hell

Oh, glorious death

Have mercy on my soul

Save me from an awful fate

Let me not grow old

Oh, glorious death

Let me fall asleep

Make that I should never wake

But yet be yours to keep

Christmas* - *December 1996

I hear the bells, ringing, ringing
And the choir's joyous singing
But these things are not for me
For happy is what I can't be
In my life there is no cheer
For I cannot have Christmas here
A time for gifts and family
Gathered 'round the Christmas tree
But I have nothing left to give
And little reason left to live

Not Human - *December 1996*

No longer human

Just a beast

Sickly gruesome

To say the least

But they don't see

What I see

The horrid monster

That is me

Fat and ugly

An experiment askew

But that is not

What they view

But I'm not human

Just a freak

And death and peace

Are all I seek

Edge of Insanity - January 1997

I am walking

On the edge of insanity.

I'm on the verge

Of losing my mind.

How long can one live

Without any dreams?

How long can one live

Without any hope?

How long does it take

For one to go mad?

I feel that I'm living

On the brink of disaster,

And soon

I'll go over the edge.

Butterfly - January 1997

The butterfly is a wonderful thing

So free and happy

Fluttering on rainbow wings

Maybe I should be a butterfly

To break from the casings of my life

Fly above the ashes

And dwindling embers of my past

Floating up on petal-tinted wings

Free to fly away

To experience the happiness of liberation

To bask in the adoration of those who see me

For I would be a thing of beauty

Yes, beautiful and pure

And full of love

Blind - ***February 1997***

Oh

How I want

To be blind

To be consumed by blackness

To be consumed by darkness

Never to see again

And in my darkness

I will not see what I am

What I have become

Or what I have been

There should be darkness

No eyes should see me

No ears should hear me

No lips should speak my name

Then I should become that darkness

Enveloped in the blackness of my soul

Becoming the blindness of all others

Never to be light again

It - February 1997

I can feel it

It eats away at my brain

It eats away at my soul

And I can see it

I see it growing in me

Changing all of me

Making me live

My own greatest fear

And it is strong

I cannot fight it

It commands the will

Of all it touches

And slowly

But surely

It kills

Ever-lasting - February 1997

I do live

In ever-lasting sadness

Wrenching pain

That feeds my madness

I do live

In ever-lasting starkness

All I see

Is ever-growing darkness

All my pain

And all my tears

Have done me nothing

All these years

You couldn't know

All the things that I knew

You couldn't live

Through all the things I lived through

I do live

In ever-lasting fear

Only wishing

That the end was near

So I could live

In ever-lasting black

And know that my pain

Would never come back

Dark: Part 2 - February 1997

Dark

Black

Empty

Cold

Pain

Hate

Fear

Wanting

Needing

Aching

Anguish

Despair

Death

Arms of Death - February 1997

Death

Oh how I wish it would embrace me

In its ever-lasting arms

To take me from this world of pain

So I would never hurt again

The end

How I want to know it

Have it take me from this place

To take me from this world of sorrow

I do not care to see tomorrow

Peace

Oh how I wish it could be mine

And that I could be free

No more knowing pain and fear

Oh how I wish the end were near

Live And Die* - *February 1997

As I live

And breath I die

There is no life

Left here inside

Far too many

Tears were shed

And all I've ever

Known is dead

I have passed

Years of time

With my words

And my rhyme

But they mean nothing

In this place

I'm just a shape

Without a face

So as I live

And breathe; I die

There is no life

Left here inside

Trapped - February 1997

Trapped

Enclosed in a meaningless form

In a meaningless life

Learning much

Yet knowing nothing

Being alive

Yet not here at all

Yes we are trapped

All earthly souls

Wandering blindly

Traveling nowhere

Living in hell

Trapped

Within ourselves

Forever

Evil Night - February 1997

The night

Grasps

And terrorizes

The dark

Breeding thoughts

Not entertained in light

Eating

The hope of life

Feeding

Your deepest despair

The evil night

Tearing your heart

Ripping your soul

Until

There is nothing left

Lust - March 1997

He gasps

At the feel

Of my nails on his back

He sighs

As my lips linger

On the point of his lust

He cries

As my hand stings

At his secret pleasure

And our bodies

Will spell out

The rhythm of lust

***Easy* - May 1997**

How easy it is

To hate you

How easy it is

To want to kill you

Cowering there in the shadows

Like the animal you are

Sneaking in the darkness

Unwilling to face

The pain you have caused

The hell you have made

The hate

That has always been yours

And as you have given

So shall you receive

For it all returns

So easy

Lif Sux - May 1997

Saw a license plate today

Said “LIF SUX”

And ain’t that the truth

Working like hell

Fighting and screaming

Crying to Devils and Gods

For our miserable lives

But those Devils and Gods

They know what they’re doing

They use us as pawns

In their deadly game

Their game of pain

Pain for the good

And bliss for the evil

Then hell after the bliss

For in this game

There are no winners

And the motto is

LIF SUX

Shades Of Grey - May 1997

All I see

Are shades of grey

The colors mingling

Blending

Until they are one

And all the same

In my eyes

And I only wish

These delicate hints

These subtle shades

Were as beautiful to you

As to me

For I am not blinded

But gifted

With sight beyond color

And these shades of grey

Are heaven

Forgotten - June 1997

The light turns dark

And the darkness fills me

And the loneliness creeps in

And takes its rightful place

Beside the dark

And fills the place

That used to be my heart

For it is empty

And it's been so long

That I've forgotten

What it is to feel

Death Alive - June 1997

Life

Is the dagger

That pierces my heart

Hate

Is the crimson

That I leave behind

Emotion

Is the axe

That opens my head

Insanity

Is the dust

That sifts from my mind

I am dead

But still alive

I am cold

Yet I survive

But why

When I am only

Death alive

I Will Not Cry - June 1997

I will not cry

Though my eyes

Are filled with tears of loneliness

I will not cry

For tears bring in the pain

And more rain

To fall down my face

But there's no place

For the pain I feel inside

So I'll fight

And believe it when I say

I can face each lonely day

And still not cry

Your Rain - June 1997

I see the lightning

And hear the roll of distant thunder

And the tears in your eyes

Are like the falling rain

And how I wish to ease your sadness

To cradle you at my heart

And fill you with joy

For you are my life

And your pain is my pain

So you should know that I love you

And I will give you all I am

To calm your storms

And end your rain

Bullet - June 1997

Bang!

The bullet breaks on through

Cracks form in the wall

The wall you built to keep you safe

Then bang!

The walls come crashing down

Your honey's on the ground

And then bang, bang!

And you too

Yes, you

Are lyin' on the floor in a pool of blood

That gunman didn't need no door

And those walls don't help you anymore

'Cause that bullet ripped right through your mind

And left a gaping hole behind

Just like that hole in society

That let the gunman have the gun

That went bang!

Pain Ends Pain - ***June 1997***

Blood

Drips from my torn and tattered flesh

Leaking out

From the places I clawed open

The self-loathing oozes out

Where I've torn myself apart

And the pain

Eases the pain

But the hate

Breeds more hate

That breeds more anger

That brings more pain

The scratches deep

The scars are white

The blood is thick

That comes from pain

That ends the pain

That brings the end

That ends us all

Bloody Hell - June 1997

Drip

Watch it drip

Dripping down

Scarlet rivers

Crimson ribbons

Cardinal carpets

To lay upon

To curl up into

While the rivulets congeal

Cover me in candy-apple love

Drench me in it

Fold me up with it

Cut me up and make me one with it

Let me taste it

Sticky copper-flavored sweetness

One last taste of heaven

As I descend into hell

Bloody hell

The Name - June 1997

Memories come

Along with the name

The name called by lovers

And those loved

Those lost

And those left behind

Those left to die

Along the side

Oh, the name

The name brings pain

From thoughts that remain

So it must die

No reason why

But it must die

Don't Want To Cry - June 1997

Don't cry

I tell myself

Don't cry

But how can I

When I just want to die

Don't want to try

And so I cry

Don't want to live

Don't want to die

Don't want to give

Don't want to try

Don't want to lie

Don't want to cry

No

I don't want to cry

Battlefield - June 1997

Life is a battlefield

The weak are left To fall upon the side

The strong are kept To fight on in the war

But war is a losing game

There are no winners

'Cause every time you try to run

The quicksand pulls you deeper

Soon your body cannot feel

But you can hear the flies buzz

And the water dripping

And vision slowly fades to haze

And the haze turns black

And the blackness consumes

And then the battlefield is empty

But must be filled with new lost souls

Unknowing of why they are here

But they are here

And the battlegrounds will live again

With new hope and new blood to shed

And we will fight on that battlefield

Until we too are weak

And will wonder

About the sweet relief

Of death

www.ingramcontent.com/pod-product-compliance
Ingram Content Group UK Ltd.
Pitfield, Milton Keynes, MK11 3LW, UK
UKHW051134260726
13967UKWH00010B/3040